Paul Fleischman

Seedfolks

AF178419

Annotations by
Mechthild Hesse

Ernst Klett Sprachen
Stuttgart

Herausgegeben von
Mechthild Hesse, Bad Homburg

1. Auflage   1 20 19 18 17 16 | 2029 28 27 26 25

Alle Drucke dieser Auflage können im Unterricht nebeneinander benutzt werden.
Die letzte Zahl bezeichnet das Jahr dieses Druckes.

Redaktion: Dr. Hartmut K. Selke
Umschlaggestaltung: Elmar Feuerbach
Umschlagbild: Alamy / © Allford Trotman
Foto des Autors S. 4: Becky Mojica
Druck: Digitaldruck Tebben GmbH, Biessenhofen

Printed in Germany.
ISBN 978-3-12-578152-8

Contents

Seedfolks

Supplementary Texts

Biographical Note

Paul Fleischman was born in Monterey, California, and grew up in Santa Monica in a family of gardeners. He attended the University of California at Berkeley and the University of New Mexico at Albuquerque. He now again lives in Monterey.

Paul Fleischman is a second-generation author: his father is Sid Fleischman, who was awarded the Newbery Medal for his book *The Whipping Boy* in 1987.

Paul is the author of numerous books for young readers, including *Joyful Noise: Poems for Two Voices,* which also won the Newbery Medal (1989).

The idea for Seedfolks came to him, he writes, when he saw "an article about a local psychotherapist who uses gardening as a therapy. [...] A stroll through a community garden leaves me happy and hopeful, cheered by the sight of what we can accomplish together." (Quoted from the HarperCollins web site).

In a letter to students in Friedrichsdorf in Germany he wrote: "That garden is fictional, but there are indeed many community gardens quite like the one I wrote about. [...] As for origins: My mother worked at a therapeutic garden for veterans; I have a friend who founded a community garden in Boston; my parents were devoted gardeners; I've worked with immigrant students ..."

Kim

I stood before our family altar. It was dawn. No one else in the apartment was awake. I stared at my father's photograph – his thin face stern, lips latched tight, his eyes peering permanently to the right. I was nine years old and still hoped that perhaps his eyes might move. Might
5 notice me.

The candles and the incense sticks, lit the day before to mark his death anniversary, had burned out. The rice and meat offered him were gone. After the evening feast, past midnight, I'd been wakened by my mother's crying. My oldest sister had joined in. My own tears had
10 then come as well, but for a different reason.

I turned from the altar, tiptoed to the kitchen and quietly drew a spoon from a drawer. I filled my lunch thermos with water and reached into our jar of dried lima beans. Then I walked outside to the street.

The sidewalk was completely empty. It was Sunday, early in April. An
15 icy wind teetered trash cans and turned my cheeks to marble. In Vietnam we had no weather like that. Here in Cleveland people call it spring. I walked half a block, then crossed the street and reached the vacant lot.

I stood tall and scouted. No one was sleeping on the old couch in the
20 middle. I'd never entered the lot before, or wanted to. I did so now, picking my way between tires and trash bags. I nearly stepped on two rats gnawing and froze. Then I told myself that I must show my bravery. I continued farther and chose a spot far from the sidewalk and hidden

---

1 **dawn** daybreak − 2 **stern** serious − 3 **to latch** to fasten with a latch *(verriegeln)* − **to peer** to look closely − 6 **incense** ['ɪnsens] substance which gives off a sweet smell when burnt *(Weihrauch)* − 7 **anniversary** [ˌænɪ'vɜːsərɪ] date exactly a year or several years after an event − 8 **feast** large meal − 9 **to join in** to start doing what s.o. else is doing − 11 **to tiptoe** to walk on the tips of one's feet − **to draw(drew, drawn)** to pull − 12 **drawer** container that slides in and out of a piece of furniture *(Schublade)* − 13 **jar** container made of glass − **lima bean** ['liːmə] kind of bean − 14 **sidewalk** *(AE)* pavement *(BE)* part of the street reserved for pedestrians − 15 **to teeter** to shake − **marble** type of hard rock *(Marmor); here:* looking like marble because of the cold − 16 **Cleveland** large industrial city in Ohio, on Lake Erie − 18 **vacant** ['veɪkənt] empty, unused − **lot** piece of land − 19 **to scout** to look around, to explore − 22 **to gnaw** [nɔː] to chew *(nagen)* − **to freeze (froze, frozen)** *here:* to stop moving − **bravery** courage − 23 **spot** place

from view by a rusty refrigerator. I had to keep my project safe.

I took out my spoon and began to dig. The snow had melted, but the ground was hard. After much work, I finished one hole, then a second, then a third. I thought about how my mother and sisters remembered
5 my father, how they knew his face from every angle and held in their fingers the feel of his hands. I had no such memories to cry over. I'd been born eight months after he'd died. Worse, he had no memories of me. When his spirit hovered over our altar, did it even know who I was?

10 I dug six holes. All his life in Vietnam my father had been a farmer. Here our apartment house had no yard. But in that vacant lot he would see me. He would watch my beans break ground and spread, and would notice with pleasure their pods growing plump. He would see my patience and my hard work. I would show him that I could raise
15 plants, as he had. I would show him that I was his daughter.

My class had sprouted lima beans in paper cups the year before. I now placed a bean in each of the holes. I covered them up, pressing the soil down firmly with my fingertips. I opened my thermos and watered them all. And I vowed to myself that those beans would thrive.

---

2 **to dig (dug, dug)** to make a hole in the ground – 5 **angle**[ˈæŋgl] *here:* point of view *(Blickwinkel)* – 8 **spirit** soul – **to hover** [ˈhɒvə] to be suspended in the air *(schweben)* – 11 **yard** *(AE)* garden *(BE)* – 12 **to spread (spread, spread)** to cover a large area – 13 **pleasure** [ˈpleʒə] feeling of happiness, satisfaction – **pod** long thin case containing seeds – **plump** fat – 14 **to raise a plant** to grow a plant – 16 **to sprout** *here:* to cause to produce new leaves, shoots – 18 **firm** strong – 19 **to vow** [vaʊ] to make a solemn promise *(geloben)* – **to thrive** to develop well *(gedeihen)*

Ana

I do love to sit and look out the window. Why do I need TV when I have forty-eight apartment windows to watch across the vacant lot, and a sliver of Lake Erie? I've seen history out this window. So much. I was four when we moved here in 1919. The fruit-sellers' carts and coal
5 wagons were pulled down the street by horses back then. I used to stand just here and watch the coal brought up by the handsome lad from Groza, the village my parents were born in. Gibb Street was mainly Rumanians back then. It was *"Adio"* – "Good-bye" – in all the shops when you left. Then the Rumanians started leaving. They weren't
10 the first, or the last. This has always been a working-class neighborhood. It's like a cheap hotel – you stay until you've got enough money to leave. A lot of Slovaks and Italians moved in next. Then Negro families in the Depression. Gibb Street became the line between the blacks and the whites, like a border between countries. I watched it happen,
15 through this very window.

I lived over in Cleveland Heights for eighteen years, then I moved back in to take care of my parents. That border moved too. Most all the whites left. Then the steel mills and factories closed and *everybody* left, like rats. Buildings abandoned. Men with no work drinking from nine
20 to five instead, down there in the lot. Always the sirens, people killing each other. Now I see families from Mexico and Cambodia and countries I don't know, twelve people sometimes in one apartment. New languages in the shops and on the street. These new people leave when they can, like the others. I'm the only one staying. It's so. Staying
25 and staring out this same window.

This spring I looked out and I saw something strange. Down in the lot, a little black-haired girl, hiding behind that refrigerator. She was working at the dirt and looking around suspiciously all the time. Then

---

3 **sliver** ['slɪvə] small, thin strip – 6 **handsome** [hænsəm] good-looking (said of a boy or man) – **lad** boy, young man – 13 **Depression** period in US history in the 1930s, when many people were unemployed – 16 **Cleveland Heights** Cleveland suburb –17 **border** line separating two areas – 18 **mill** building where raw materials are processed *(Fabrik)* – 19 **to abandon** [əˈbændən] to leave, give up – **from nine to five** the usual working day – 28 **suspicious** expecting s.th. bad to happen

I realized. She was burying something. I never had children of my own, but I've seen enough in that lot to know she was mixed up in something she shouldn't be. And after twenty years typing for the Parole department, I just about knew what she'd buried. Drugs most likely, or
5　money, or a gun. The next moment, she disappeared like a rabbit.

I thought of calling up the police. Then I saw her there the next morning, and I decided I'd solve this case myself. We had a long spell of rain then. I didn't set eyes on her once. Then the weather turned warm and I saw her twice more, always in the morning, on her way to
10　school. She was crouched down with her back to me so I couldn't see just what she was doing. My curiosity was like a fever inside me. Then one morning she was there, glancing about, and she looked straight up at this window. I pulled my head back behind the curtain. I wasn't sure if she'd seen me. If she had, she wouldn't leave her treasure buried
15　long. Then I knew I'd have to dig it up before she did.

I waited an hour after she left. Then I took an old butter knife and my cane and hobbled down all three flights of stairs. I worked my way through that awful jungle of junk and finally came to her spot. I stooped down. It was wet there and easy digging. I hacked and dug, but didn't
20　find anything, except for a large white bean. I tried a new spot and found another, then a third. Then the truth of it slapped me full in the face. I said to myself, "What have you *done*?" Two beans had roots. I knew I'd done them harm. I felt like I'd read through her secret diary and had ripped out a page without meaning to. I laid those beans right
25　back in the ground, as gently as sleeping babies. Then I patted the soil as smooth as could be.

The next morning she was back. I peeked around the curtain. She didn't look up here or give any sign that she noticed something wrong. I could see her clearly this time. She reached a hand into her schoolbag.
30　Then she pulled out a jar, unscrewed the lid, and poured out water onto the ground.

That afternoon I bought some binoculars.

---

1 **to bury** ['berı] to hide s.th. in the ground – 3 **parole department** [pə'rəʊl]
Bewährungsabteilung – 7 **to solve a case** to find the answer to a problem – **spell**
period of time – 10 **to crouch** to lower the body by bending the knees – 12 **to glance about**
to look around – 17 **cane** walking stick– 18 **junk** worthless things that people throw
away – **to stoop down** to bend forward and down – 24 **to mean** *here:* to want –
26 **smooth** [smu:ð] even, not rough – 27 **to peek at** to have a quick and secret look –
30 **to unscrew a lid** to open a closed jar

Wendell

My phone doesn't ring much, which suits me fine. That's how I got the news about our boy, shot dead like a dog in the street. And the word, last year, about my wife's car wreck. I can't hear a phone and not jerk inside. When Ana called I was still asleep. Phone calls that wake me up
5 are the worst.

"Get up here quick!" she says. I live on the ground floor and watch out for her a little. We're the only white people left in the building. I ran up the stairs. I could tell it was serious. I prayed I wouldn't find her dead. When I got there, she looked perfectly fine. She dragged me over
10 to the window. "Look down there!" she says. "They're dying!"

"What?" I yelled back.

"The plants!" she says.

I was mad. She gave me some binoculars and told me all about the Chinese girl. I found the plants and got them in focus. There were four
15 of them in a row, still little. They were wilted. Leaves flopped flat on the ground.

"What are they?" she asked.

"Some kind of beans." I grew up on a little farm in Kentucky. "But she planted 'em way too early. She's lucky those seeds even came up."
20 "But they did," said Ana. "And it's up to us to save them."

It was a weekend in May and hot. You'd have thought that those beans were hers. They needed water, especially in that heat. She said the girl hadn't come in four days – sick, probably, or gone out of town. Ana had twisted her ankle and couldn't manage the stairs. She pointed
25 to a pitcher. "Fill that up and soak them good. Quick now."

School janitors take too much bossing all week to listen to an extra helping on weekends. I stared at her one long moment, then took my time about filling the pitcher.

---

1 **it suits me fine** I like it that way – 3 **car wreck** [rek] car accident – **to jerk** [dʒɜːk] to move suddenly – 9 **to drag** to pull along – 13 **mad** angry – 14 **in focus** adjusted (camera, binoculars) so s.th. can be seen clearly – 15 **wilted** almost dried *(verwelkt)* – **to flop** to fall heavily – 18 **Kentucky** state in the eastern U.S. – 20 **it's up to us** it is our duty – 24 **to twist one's ankle** *sich den Knöchel verstauchen* – 25 **pitcher** large jug *(Kanne)* – **to soak** to make wet – 26 **janitor** *(AE)* person who looks after a building – **to take much bossing** to be ordered around in an arrogant manner – **extra helping** more of s.th. *(Extraportion)*

I walked down the stairs and into the lot and found the girl's plants. You don't plant beans till the weather's hot. Then I saw what had kept her seeds from freezing. The refrigerator in front of them had bounced the sunlight back on the soil, heating it up like an oven. I bent down
5 and gave the dirt a feel. It was hard packed and light colored. I studied the plants. Leaves shaped like spades in a deck of cards. Definitely beans. I scraped up a ring of dirt around the first plant, to hold the water and any rain that fell. I picked up the pitcher and poured the water slowly. Then I heard something move and spun around. The girl
10 was there, stone-still, ten feet away, holding her own water jar.

She hadn't seen me behind the refrigerator. She looked afraid for her life. Maybe she thought I'd jump up and grab her. I gave her a smile and showed her that I was just giving her plants some water. This made her eyes go even bigger. I stood up slowly and backed away. I smiled again.
15 She watched me leave. We never spoke one word.

I walked back there that evening and checked on the beans. They'd picked themselves up and were looking fine. I saw that she'd made a circle of dirt around the other three plants. Out of nowhere the words from the Bible came into my head: "And a little child shall lead them. "
20 I didn't know why at first. Then I did. There's plenty about my life I can't change. Can't bring the dead back to life on this earth. Can't make the world loving and kind. Can't change myself into a millionaire. But a patch of ground in this trashy lot – I *can* change that. Can change it big. Better to put my time into that than moaning about the other all day.
25 That little grammar-school girl showed me that.

The lot had buildings on three sides. I walked around and picked myself out a spot that wouldn't be shaded too much. I dragged the garbage off to the side and tossed out the biggest pieces of broken glass. I looked over my plot, squatted down, and fingered the soil
30 awhile.

That Monday I brought a shovel home from work.

---

3 **to bounce back** to reflect – 6 **spade** *here:* group of playing cards *(Pik)* – **deck of cards** pack of playing cards – 12 **to jump s.o.** to attack s.o. – **to grab** to get hold of – 23 **patch** *here:* a small area – **trashy** untidy, full of things thrown away – 24 **to moan** to complain loudly *(stöhnen)* – 22 **shaded** protected from the heat of the sun – 23 **to toss** out to throw away – 24 **to squat** [skwɒt] to sit on one's feet – 31 **shovel** [ˈʃʌvəl] tool for digging up sand *(Schaufel)*

Gonzalo

The older you are, the younger you get when you move to the United
States.

They don't teach that equation in school. Big Brain, Mr. Smoltz, my
eighth-grade math teacher, hasn't even heard of it. It's not in *Gateway
to Algebra*. It's Garcia's Equation. I'm the Garcia.

Two years after my father and I moved here from Guatemala I could
speak English. I learned it on the playground and watching lots of TV.
Don't believe what people say – cartoons make you *smart*. But my
father, he worked all day in a kitchen with Mexicans and Salvadorans.
His English was worse than a kindergartner's. He would only buy food
at the *bodega* down the block. Outside of there he lowered his eyes and
tried to get by on mumbles and smiles. He didn't want strangers to
hear his mistakes. So he used me to make phone calls and to talk to the
landlady and to buy things in stores where you had to use English. He
got younger. I got older.

Then my younger brothers and mother and Tío Juan, her uncle,
came north and joined us. Tío Juan was the oldest man in his pueblo.
But here he became a little baby. He'd been a farmer, but here he
couldn't work. He couldn't sit out in the plaza and talk – there *aren't* any
plazas here, and if you sit out in public some gang driving by might use
you for target practice. He couldn't understand TV. So he wandered
around the apartment all day, in and out of rooms, talking to himself,
just like a kid in diapers.

One morning he wandered outside and down the street. My mother
practically fainted. He doesn't speak Spanish, just an Indian language.
I finally found him standing in front of the beauty parlor, staring

---

3 **equation** mathematical statement that says that two parts have the same value
(Gleichung) – 4 **gateway** entrance – 6 **Guatemala** country in Central America – 8 **cartoon**
animated cartoon as shown on TV – 9 **Salvadoran** citizen from El Salvador (country in
Central America) – 10 **kindergartner** a child in a kinder-garten – 11 **bodega** *Spanish:*
shop/restaurant – 12 **to get by on mumbles and smiles** to survive by just uttering
sounds and smiling – 14 **landlady** woman who owns the house in which you live –
17 **pueblo** *Spanish:* village – 19 **plaza** *Spanish:* town square – 21 **target practice** practice
shooting – 23 **diaper** [ˈdaɪəpə] *(AE)* baby's nappy *(Windel)* – 25 **to faint** to fall to the
ground unconscious – 26 **beauty parlor** shop where women's faces, hair, nails etc are
looked after

through the glass at a woman with a drier over her head. He must have wondered what weird planet he'd moved to. I led him home, holding his hand, the way you would with a three-year-old. Since then I'm supposed to baby-sit him after school.

5　　One afternoon I was watching TV, getting smart on *The Brady Bunch*. Suddenly I looked up. He was gone. I checked the halls on all five floors of the apartment house. I ran to the street. He wasn't in the *bodega* or the pawnshop. I called his name, imagining my mother's face when she found out he'd fallen through a manhole or been run over. I turned

10　the corner, looking for the white straw hat he always wore. Two blocks down I spotted it. I flew down the sidewalk and found him standing in front of a vacant lot, making gestures to a man with a shovel.

I took his hand, but he pulled me through the trash and into the lot. I recognized the man with the shovel – he was the janitor at my old

15　school. He had a little garden planted. Different shades of green leaves were coming up in rows. Tío Juan was smiling and trying to tell him something. The man couldn't understand him and finally went back to digging. I turned Tío Juan around and led him home.

That night he told my mother all about it. She was the only one who

20　could understand him. When she got home from work the next day she asked me to take him back there. I did. He studied the sun. Then the soil. He felt it, then smelled it, then actually tasted it. He chose a spot not too far from the sidewalk. Where my mother changed busses she'd gone into a store and bought him a trowel and four packets of seeds. I

25　cleared the trash, he turned the soil. I wished we were farther from the street and I was praying that none of my friends or girlfriends or enemies saw me. Tío Juan didn't even notice people – he was totally wrapped up in the work.

He showed me exactly how far apart the rows should be and how

30　deep. He couldn't read the words on the seed packets, but he knew from the pictures what seeds were inside. He poured them into his

---

5 **The Brady Bunch** popular TV series about an American family – 8 **pawnshop** ['pɔːnʃɒp] shop where money is lent for people's belongings *(Pfandleiher)* – 9 **manhole** hole in the street that gives access to the sewers (usu. covered by an iron lid) – 11 **to spot** to notice, to see – 12 **to make gestures** ['dʒestʃəz] to move one's body to make oneself understood – 24 **trowel** ['traʊəl] small handheld tool with a flat pointed blade *(Handschaufel)* – 28 **to be wrapped** [ræpt] **up in** to be absorbed in

hand and smiled. He seemed to recognize them, like old friends. Watching him carefully sprinkling them into the troughs he'd made, I realized that I didn't know anything about growing food and that he knew everything. I stared at his busy fingers, then his eyes. They were

5 focused, not faraway or confused. He'd changed from a baby back into a man.

2 **trough** [trɒf] shallow hole – 5 **focused** *here:* clearly directed at s.th.

Leona

Mama believed in doctors, but not Granny. Not even if they were black.
No, ma'am. I grew up in her house, back in Atlanta. She drank down a
big cup of goldenrod tea every morning, with a nutmeg floating in it,
and declared she didn't need no other medicine. Dr. Bates tried to sell
5 her his iron pills and told her straight out that that tea of hers would
raise her blood pressure and burst her heart. He passed away that very
same summer. Next doctor said it would give her brain fever. He died
on his fiftieth birthday, I believe, right during the party. Had him a real
nice funeral, later. Granny lived to ninety-nine by her count. She kept
10 a scrapbook with the obituaries of all the doctors she outlived and
could recite the list of names by heart, like a chapter out of Genesis. We
took to going to their funerals right regular over the years. She always
laid some goldenrod on their graves.

I was thinking about her one day, walking home from the grocery
15 store on Gibb Street. Then I came to the vacant lot and saw three
people in different parts of it. I thought maybe they were looking for
money. Turned out they had shovels, not metal detectors. When I saw
they had little gardens going, I said to myself, "I believe I'll plant me a
patch of goldenrod right here."

20 There was a man standing and watching from the sidewalk and a girl
looking down out a window. There were probably lots of folks who'd
want to grow something, just like me. Then I studied all the trash on
the ground. Don't know why anyone called that lot "vacant." The
garbage was piled high as your waist, some of it from the neighborhood
25 and some dropped off by outside people. The ones who don't want to
pay at the dump, or got dangerous chemicals, or think we're such slobs

---

2 **Atlanta** biggest city in Georgia (southern U.S. state) – 3 **goldenrod** plant with small
yellow flowers that bloom in late summer (Goldrute) – **nutmeg** *Muskatnuss* – 6 **to
pass away** to die – 9 **funeral** burial of a dead person – 10 **scrapbook** book with blank
pages in which you can paste newspaper clippings – **obituary** [əʊˈbɪtʃʊərɪ] notice of a
person's death – **to outlive s.o.** to live longer than – 11 **to recite** [rɪˈsaɪt] **by heart** to
repeat aloud from memory – **Genesis** [ˈdʒenəsɪs] first book of the Bible – 12 **to take
to** to start doing s.th. regularly – 24 **garbage** rubbish, junk *(Müll, Dreck)* – **to pile** to
make a little heap (anhäufen) – **waist** part of the body below the ribs and above the
hips *(Taille)* – 26 **dump** area where garbage is deposited (Müllkippe) – **slob** untidy
person

down here we won't mind another load of junk. We can't get City Hall to *pick up* our trash, but we got it *delivered* just fine. The smell's enough to curl up a crocodile's nose, especially in the summer. The gardeners had made some trails through it. But I knew precious few would join
5 'em until that mess was hauled away. Looking at it, I knew this wasn't a job for no wheelbarrow. This was a job for the telephone.

I marched on home. I've got two kids in a high school that has more guns than books, so I know all about complaining to officials and such about things that need changing. Next morning was Monday. At nine
10 o'clock I drank me a tall glass of water. I knew I'd be having to say the same thing to fifteen or twenty government folks. I put Miles on the CD player and stretched out on the bed. Might as well be comfortable when you're on hold. Then I opened the phone book and started in dialing.
15 You ever watch a sax player close? They push down a key and way at the other end of the instrument something moves. That's what I was looking for – the key that would make that trash disappear. I tried the City of Cleveland, then Cuyahoga County, then the State of Ohio, and finally the U.S. government. Six and a half hours later I found out the
20 lot was owned by the city. But the people running Cleveland don't usually come down here, unless they take a wrong turn on the freeway. You can't measure the distance between my block and City Hall in miles.

Just the same, I kept working on it the next day. That Citizens'
25 Information Center told me to call the Public Health Department. They sent me to someone else. They're all trained to be slippery as snakes. And to be out to lunch, to not return messages, and to keep folks on hold till they get gray and die. I had the feeling I was getting farther from the key I needed instead of closer. Then on the third day,

---

1 **City Hall** town hall, the building housing the city government; *here:* the local government itself – 2 **to deliver** bring *(liefern)* – 3 **to curl up** to cause to roll up – 4 **trail** path – **precious** [preʃəs] **few** *(coll.)* very few – 5 **to haul s.th. away** to carry s.th. off – 6 **wheelbarrow** small cart with one wheel and two handles *(Schubkarre)* – 8 **to complain** to protest – **officials** people working for the government – **and such** and people like that – 11 **Miles** Miles Davis (1926 - 1991) famous jazz trumpeter – 13 **to be on hold** to be waiting (on the phone) – 18 **Cuyahoga County** county surrounding Cleveland – 20 **to run** *here:* to govern – 21 **unless** if not – 22 **to measure** [mɛʒə] to find out the exact distance or size *(messen)* – 24 **just the same** nevertheless – 26 **slippery** *here:* not direct *(aalglatt)*

I thought on it. When people talk to you on the phone, you're nothing but a voice. And when you're on hold you're not even that. I had to make myself real to 'em.

That morning I took a bus downtown and walked into the Public
5 Health Department. Told about the trash all over again to this dolled-up receptionist. Let her see me up close and personal and hear me loud and clear. She just told me to sit down with the others waiting. I did. Then I opened the garbage bag I'd picked up in the lot on my way.

10 The smell that came out of it made you think of hog pens and maggots and kitchen scraps from back when Nixon was president. It was amazing how quick people noticed it, including that receptionist. And even more amazing how quick I was called in to have a meeting with someone. I was *definitely* real to them now. I brought that bag
15 along with me into the meeting, to keep it that way.

---

5 **dolled-up** dressed up – 6 **receptionist** person whose job it is to welcome guests – 10 **hog pen** place where pigs are kept – 11 **maggot** larva which eventually turns into a fly – **kitchen scraps** food remains – **Nixon** Richard Nixon, 37th U.S. president (1969-1974) – 14 **definitely** ['defɪnɪtlɪ] certainly

Sam

I saw people on the sidewalk, watching something. I crossed to join
them, like a cat who smells herring. Men in jumpsuits, from the jail I
think, were clearing the lot. Unbelievable. The woman beside me told
me the land was for anyone who wanted a garden. Even more
5 unbelievable. The word "paradise" came out of my mouth, without
thinking. The woman looked at me strange. It's a hobby with me,
studying words. I looked at the three walls surrounding the lot, then at
a garden coming up beautiful, planted there close to the sidewalk.
"Paradise" comes from a Persian word. It means "walled park." I told
10 the woman that. This time she gave me a little smile. I smiled back.
That's my occupation.

You've seen fishermen mending the rips in their nets. That's what I
do, only with people. I used to try to patch up the whole world. For
thirty-six years I worked for different groups, promoting world
15 government, setting up conferences on pacifism, raising money,
stuffing envelopes. Not that I've given up the fight. I've just switched
battlefields, from the entire planet to this corner of Cleveland.
Sometimes I think I've actually had more effect on the world since I
retired. What do I do? I smile at people, especially black people and the
20 ones from different countries. I get 'em looking up at me instead of
down or off to the side. I start up conversations in lines and on the bus
and with cashiers. People see I'm friendly, no matter what they've
heard about whites or Jews. If I'm lucky, I get 'em talking to each other.
Sewing up the rip in the neighborhood.

25 I hadn't had a garden since I was a kid. I wanted one now, only this
time I was seventy-eight to be exact, and in no condition to dig up the
soil. So I hired a teenager, Puerto Rican, who said he knew where he
could get a shovel. He knew he'd have to do a good job to be paid. He
worked that soil until it flowed through your fingers like silk. I paid him

---

2 **jumpsuit** overall – 11 **occupation** here: job – 12 **to mend** to repair –13 **to patch up** to
repair– 14 **to promote** *here:* to fight for – 15 **to set up** to arrange – **to raise money** to
collect money – 16 **to stuff** to fill – **to switch** to change from one place to the next –
17 **entire** [ɪn'taɪə] whole – 19 **to retire** [rɪ'taɪə] to end one's working life – 21 **in lines** in
queues – 22 **cashier** [kæ'ʃɪə] person in shop who takes your money – 24 **to sew** [səʊ]
to work with a needle and thread; *here:* to mend, to repair – **rip** a torn part *(Riss)* – 27
to hire [haɪə] to employ, to pay – 29 **silk** very soft and smooth material (Seide)

well and offered him a row. He wanted to grow marijuana, to sell. A real businessman. We discussed this. We finally compromised on pumpkins, after I explained how much he could probably get for them at Halloween, not to mention the advantages of staying out of jail. He was
5 new to the neighborhood. We chatted back and forth. Squatting there in the cool of the evening, planting our seeds, a few other people working, a robin singing out strong all the while, it seemed to me that we were in truth in Paradise, a small Garden of Eden.

In the Bible, though, there's a river in Eden. Here, we had none. Not
10 even a spigot anywhere close by. Nothing. People had to lug their own water, in buckets or milk jugs or soda containers. Water is heavy as bricks, trust me. And new seeds have to be always moist. And in all of June it didn't rain but four days. The result? People bent over like coolies, walking sometimes three or four blocks, a gallon jug in each
15 hand, complaining all the time about the water. Mine I had hauled by a third-grader with a wagon. The contest I started came later.

Water aside, we had other problems. People in the garden told friends and relatives. The lot was big, there was plenty of room. But when newcomers joined, at least at the beginning, they could usually
20 get a spot near people they knew. One Saturday, when the garden was fullest, I stood up a minute to straighten my back. And what did I see? With a few exceptions, the blacks on one side, the whites on another, the Central Americans and Asians toward the back. The garden was a copy of the neighborhood. I guess I shouldn't have been surprised. A
25 duck gives birth to a duckling, not a moose. Each group kept to itself, spoke its own language, and grew its own special crops. One man even put up a pole and flew the Philippine flag above his plot.

Then there was the garbage. A few well brought-up people in the buildings around the lot still used it for a trash can. Just couldn't get out

---

7 **robin** black American bird with a red breast *(turdus migratorius)* – 10 **spigot** ['spɪgət] valve (Ventil) for controlling the flow of water, tap – **to lug** to carry (s.th. heavy) – 12 **moist** a bit wet *(feucht)* – 13 **it didn't rain but four days** it only rained on four days – 14 **coolie** unskilled worker (usu. one living in China) – **gallon jug** a container holding a gallon (= c. 3.8 liters) – 16 **contest** competition – 25 **moose** [muːs] large animal that lives in northern regions *(Elch)* – 26 **crops** farm products grown in the soil – 29 **to get out of the habit** to act differently than one is used to

of the habit. They emptied their ashtrays out the windows and tossed out all sorts of stuff. One day a bottle came down, like a meteor. A man picked it up and threw it back, straight through the window it came out of. A minute later, five more flew out. Next, I thought to myself, come
5 gunshots. Instead, thank God, it was only shouting.

That crazy homeless man, the one who used to sleep on the broken-down couch – he also missed the lot being a dump. He showed up, saw his couch had been taken, and started ripping out people's plants. The police had to come. Some people started worrying, looking ahead to
10 ripe beans and tomatoes and thinking about strangers coming in. That week, a man put chicken wire around his garden, five feet high, complete with a little gate and padlock. The week after that someone built a board fence. Then came the first KEEP OUT sign. Then, the crowning achievement – barbed wire.
15 God, who made Eden, also wrecked the Tower of Babel, by dividing people. From Paradise, the garden was turning back into Cleveland.

---

11 **chicken wire** ['waɪə] a fence made of wire mesh *(Drahtzaun)* – 12 **padlock** a removable lock *(Vorhängeschloss)* – 13 **board fence** fence made of wood *(Bretterzaun)* – 14 **crowning achievement** climax *(krönender Abschluss)* – **barbed wire** metal wire with short, sharp points *(Stacheldraht)*

Virgil

My father, he always has a smile on his face and a plan moving in his head. We were standing together on the sidewalk while the men were clearing the lot. I was watching the rats running for their lives. They were shooting off every which way. A couple of dealers came over, the
5 ones always bragging about how bad they are. A rat ran right up one of their legs. The dude screamed, just like women do with a mouse in cartoons, only louder. Shook his leg like his toe was being electrocuted. That rat flew off and dove down a storm drain. I looked at my father. That's when I saw that he hadn't paid the rat any mind. Hadn't even
10 turned his head. His eyes were stuck completely on the garden land being uncovered. He had a two-foot-wide smile on his face.

My father drove a bus back in Haiti. Here he drives a taxi. That night he drove himself way across town to borrow two shovels from a friend of his. The next morning was the first day without school. I was done
15 with fifth grade forever. I'd planned on sleeping till noon to celebrate. But when it was still half dark my father shook my shoulder. School was over, but that garden was just starting.

We walked down and picked out a place to dig up. The ground was packed so hard, the tip of my shovel bounced off it like a pogo stick. We
20 tried three spots till we found one we liked. Then we walked back and forth, picking out broken glass, like chickens pecking seeds. After that we turned the soil. We were always digging up more trash – bolts and screws and pieces of brick. That's how I found the locket. It was shaped like a heart and covered with rust, with a broken chain. I got it open.
25 Inside was this tiny photo of a girl. She was white, with a sad-looking face. She had on this hat with flowers on it. I don't know why I kept it

---

4 **to shoot off** to run away – **dealer** person who sells drugs – 5 **to brag** to talk about o.s. with too much pride *(angeben)* – 6 **dude** *(informal AE)* man – 7 **to be electrocuted** to die or be badly injured after touching electric wires – 8 **to dive (dove, dove)** to go under water, to take cover – **drain** water pipe – 9 **mind** *here:* attention – 13 **way** *here:* all the way; very far – 19 **to bounce off** to be pushed back – **pogo stick** toy stick on which you jump up and down on the ground – 22 **bolt** *Bolzen* – 23 **screw** [skru:] *Schraube* – **brick** red-brown piece of burnt clay used for building walls – **locket** piece of a necklace in which you can keep the picture of a person you love

instead of tossing it on our trash pile.

It seemed like hours and hours before we had the ground finished. We rested a while. Then my father asked if I was ready. I thought he meant ready to plant our seeds. But instead, we turned another square of ground. Then another after that. Then three more after that. My father hadn't been smiling to himself about some little garden. He was thinking of a farm, to make money. I'd seen a package of seeds for pole beans and hoped that's what we'd grow. They get so tall that the man in the picture was picking 'em way at the top of a ladder. But my father said no. He was always asking people in his cab about how to get rich. One of 'em told him that fancy restaurants paid lots of money for this baby lettuce, smaller than the regular kind, to use in rich folks' salads. The fresher it was, the higher the price. My father planned to pick it and then race it right over in his cab. Running red lights if he had to.

Lettuce seeds are smaller than sand. I felt embarrassed, planting so much ground. No one else's garden was a quarter the size of ours. Suddenly I saw Miss Fleck. I hardly recognized her in jeans. She was the strictest teacher in Ohio. I'd had her for third grade. She pronounced every letter in every word, and expected you to talk the same way. She was tall and even blacker than my father. No slouching in your seat in her class or any kind of rudeness. The other teachers seemed afraid of her too. She walked over just when we finished planting.

"Well, Virgil," she said. "You seem to have claimed quite a large *plantation* here."

That's just what I was afraid of hearing. I looked away from her, down at our sticks. We'd put 'em in the ground and run string around 'em, cutting our land up into six pieces. I didn't know why, till my father stepped forward.

"Actually, madam, only this very first area here is ours," he said. He had on his biggest smile. He must have remembered her. "The others

---

1 **to toss** to throw – 10 **cab** taxi – 11 **fancy** expensive, elegant – 12 **lettuce** [lɛtɪs] green leaves used in salads, etc. *(Kopfsalat)* – 14 **to run red lights** to drive on although the traffic lights are red – 20 **to slouch** [slaʊtʃ] to sit in a careless way – 21 **rudeness** impolite behavior– 23 **to claim s.th.** to say that s.th. (esp. a piece of land) belongs to you – 26 **string** thin cord used for tying things together *(Kordel)*

we have planted at the request of relatives who have no tools or who live too far."

"Really, now," said Miss Fleck.

"Yes, madam," said my father. He pointed at the closest squares of
5 land. "My brother Antoine. My auntie, Anne-Marie."

My eyes opened wide. They both lived in Haiti. I stared at my father, but he just kept smiling. His fingers pointed farther to the left. "My Uncle Philippe." He lived in New York. "My wife's father." He died last year. "And her sister." I looked at my father's smiling face. I'd never
10 watched an adult lie before.

"And what did your *extended* family of gardeners ask you to plant?" said Miss Fleck.

"Lettuce," said my father. "All lettuce."

"What a coincidence," she said back. She just stood, then walked
15 over to her own garden. I'm pretty sure she didn't believe him. But what principal could she send him to?

That lettuce was like having a new baby in the family. And I was like its mother. I watered it in the morning if my father was still out driving. It was supposed to come up in seven days, but it didn't. My father
20 couldn't figure out why. Neither of us knew anything about plants. This wrinkled old man in a straw hat tried to show me something when I poured out the water. He spoke some language, but it sure wasn't English. I didn't get what he was babbling about, till the lettuce finally came up in wavy lines and bunches instead of straight rows. I'd washed
25 the seeds out of their places.

The minute it came up, it started to wilt. It was like a baby always crying for its milk. I got sick of hauling bottles of water in our shopping cart, like I was some old lady. Then the heat came. The leaves shriveled up. Some turned yellow. That lettuce was dying.
30 My father practically cried, looking at it. He'd stop by in his cab when he could, with two five-gallon water containers riding in the back instead of passengers. Then bugs started eating big holes in the plants. I couldn't see anyone buying them from us. My father had promised we'd make enough money to buy me an eighteen-speed bike. I was

---

1 **at the request of s.o.** because s.o. has asked you to do s.th. – 11 **extended family** the family including grandparents, uncles, etc. – 14 **What a coincidence.** [ˌkəʊˈɪnsɪdəns] What a surprise! How strange! *(Welch ein Zufall!)* – 16 **principal** (AE) headmaster – 21 **wrinkled** full of creases or folds *(faltig)* – 24 **wavy** not straight, with waves *(gewellt)* – 26 **to wilt** to lose strength *(welken)* – 28 **to shrivel** [ˈʃrɪvl] to become dry – 32 **bug** insect – 34 **speed** "gear" of a bike *(Gang)*

counting on it. I'd already told my friends. My father asked all his passengers what to do. His cab was like a library for him. Finally, one of 'em told him that spring or fall was the time to grow lettuce, that the summer was too hot for it. My father wasn't smiling when he told us.

5   I couldn't believe it. I stomped outside. I could feel that eighteen-speed slipping away. I was used to seeing kids lying and making mistakes, but not grown-ups. I was mad at my father. Then I sort of felt sorry for him.

    That night I pulled out the locket. I opened it up and looked at the
10 picture. We'd studied Greek myths in school that year. In our book, the goddess of crops and the earth had a sad mouth and flowers around her, just like the girl in the locket. I scraped off the rust with our dish scrubber and shined up that locket as bright as I could get it. Then I opened it up, just a crack. Then I whispered, "Save our lettuce," to the
15 girl.

---

5 **to stomp** to put one's feet down with force – 10 **myth** [mɪθ] tale about gods and heroes *(Sage)* – 12 **to scrape off** to take s.th. away by passing a sharp object over s.th. *(abkratzen)* – 13 **scrubber** stiff brush

Sae Young

Always many people in my house when I was young. Five sisters. Many friends. I always like being with people. Then I leave Korea with my husband to come to America, for work. We buy dry cleaning shop, live next block. Dry cleaning shop better than restaurant. Don't have to
5 speak English too much and only work six days. We work together, seven until seven. At night I sew alterations. We save all for children's college, so they can have easier life. But no children come. Very many years we hope, but still alone. Then my husband die. Heart attack. Thirty-seven years old. Now all alone, except for friends. I hire woman
10 to work in shop. One afternoon when she gone, a man walk into shop with coat to clean. Under coat he has gun. He take out money, then push me down. He yelling at me. Very bad words. Then he kick me. Break cheekbone. Then he kick me again, head hit hard against wall and I go to sleep.
15 When I wake up, I no more like to be with people, like before. Afraid of everyone, all the time. I don't leave apartment for two months. Neighbor buys food for me at store. I don't open door if someone knocks, even friends – only for food. Afraid to walk on sidewalk with people. I hire Korean man to run dry cleaning shop. I never go in. That
20 happen two years ago. Very slowly, I get better. I go to store and buy my food, but very fast. Then not so fast. Very lonely, but still afraid. Then I pass by garden.

Vietnamese girl was working there, picking beautiful lima beans. A man and a woman on other side, talking over row of corn. Hear man
25 say his wife give him hoe for birthday. I want to be with people again. Next day I go back and dig small garden. Nobody talk to me that day. But just be near people, nice people, feel good, like next to fire in winter.

Very hot and humid in July. Most people come early in evening, after
30 work, when air is cool. People watering and pulling weeds. Even if don't talk to anyone, sound of people working almost like conversation,

---

3 **dry cleaning shop** shop where clothes are cleaned – 6 **sew** [səʊ] to work with needle and thread *(nähen)* – **alteration** change *(Änderung)* – 13 **cheekbone** bone under the eye – 25 **hoe** garden tool used to loosen the ground and to remove unwanted plants *(Hacke)* – 29 **humid** ['hjuːmɪd] damp, moist – 30 **to pull weeds** to take out wild unwanted plants

all around. People visit friends. I listen to voices. Feel very safe. Then man walk over and ask about peppers. I grow hot peppers, like in Korea. First time that someone talk to me. I was so glad, have trouble talking.

5 That man named Sam. He's American man and talk to everyone. Very smart. When people all the time complain about carrying water, he start contest. He said how adults couldn't solve problem, let children try. He say he give twenty dollars to child under twelve who has best idea. He write this on paper and nail paper to post close to sidewalk.

10 One week to contest. Kids out of school, walk around, see paper, tell friends. On Saturday, everyone bring plans. Sam has wooden box, let each one stand on it and tell idea. One girl live in apartment by garden. She say she'll open window, people give her containers, she'll fill them with water. Then mother interrupt, say water bill too much. Boy say 15 use water from fire hydrant. Another say run hose from Lake Erie. Many ideas. Sam explain how much money each one cost. Then little black girl say to let rain from spouts go into garbage cans. Everyone look. Three different spouts on walls of building around garden. Just have to take off bottom part of spout. Sam give girl twenty dollars. 20 Everyone clap. Other people give money to buy garbage cans.

Next day, thunderstorm. Cans almost full. Little girl there, very proud. Someone bring three old pots to scoop water out of cans. Hard to pour into narrow containers. I quick go to store. Buy three funnels to make much easier filling containers. I put one by each garbage can. 25 That day I see man use my funnel. Then woman. Then many people. Feel very glad inside. Feel part of garden. Almost like family.

---

2 **pepper** *Paprika* – 15 **hose** [hə∪z] long, flexible pipe (Schlauch) – 17 **spout** [spa∪t] *here:* pipe through which rainwater comes down from roofs – 22 **to scoop** to take out with a kind of big spoon – 25 **funnel** cone-shaped object for filling water, etc. into bottles *(Trichter)*

Curtis

Deltoids – awesome. Pecs – check 'em out. Quads – now playing on a body near you. Can't help being born with this body, or living three doors down from Kapp's Gym. Can't stop people calling me Atlas or Ceps. That's short for Biceps R Us. Actually, I started that name. But
5 that was before Lateesha cut me loose.

We had us a real nice thing going. She was a few years older than me, always talking about having a family, living in a house in the country, like her aunt's place in Michigan. I wasn't really listening too hard. I was twenty-three. With this body, I had other girls hanging on me at
10 the time. Some of 'em I just couldn't brush off. When Lateesha found out, she slammed the door in my face so hard the paint cracked.

You don't know what you got till it's gone. All that was five years ago. I've caught up with her now. Done fooling around. She was looking for a husband, and now I'm looking for a wife. I moved back from Cincinnati
15 in May and ran into her brother the first day. Said she's still single. Same third-floor apartment. But when I came up to her on the street, she turned her back. Wouldn't let me explain. Twice it happened. No chance for words. So I decided to give her some deeds instead.

She lives straight across the street from the garden. I staked out a
20 spot right by the sidewalk, where she could look down and see it. Then I came home with six little tomato plants in plastic containers. She had a serious thing for tomatoes. She'd put a monster slice on a piece of bread and call it a sandwich. She'd even bite into 'em, just like apples. Always talking about eating 'em out of her aunt's garden when she was
25 a kid and how she wanted to grow 'em someday. She probably thought

---

1 **deltoid** [ˈdeltɔɪd] triangular shoulder muscle – **awesome** great, wonderful – **pecs** pectoral muscles, i.e. muscles of the chest – **to check s.th. out** to try s.th. out – **quad** [kwɒd] (muscle) having four sides – 3 **gym** gymnsasium, place where you do exercises – **Atlas** in Greek mythology a titan holding the sky on his shoulders (in pictures Atlas is usually shown holding the earth) – 4 **Ceps** nickname (from biceps) – **Biceps R Us** word play on the toy store Toys R Us – 5 **to cut loose** [luːs] (slang) to send away, to say that a relationship is over – 8 **Michigan** [ˈmɪʃɪɡən] U.S. state in the Midwest – 13 **to catch up with s.o.** to meet s.o. again – **done fooling around** (slang) I have finished dating lots of different girls – 18 **deed** s.th. one does (not just words; cf. the proverb "Deeds speak louder than words." – 19 **to stake out** to claim (land) as one's own

I forgot all that. I planted 'em right there in front of her eyes, to show her I hadn't, that I was waiting for her.

I got the biggest – beefsteak tomatoes. I could see 'em in my mind, bright as traffic lights, flashing at her across the street. I'd never grown
5   anything before. I got into it. Every day something new. The first flower bud. Then those first yellow flowers. Then the tomatoes growing right behind 'em. This old man with no teeth and a straw hat showed me how to tie the plants up to stakes. Then someone else told me all their diseases. That got me worrying. What if all my plants started wilting?
10 Or caught blight and died? That wasn't any message I'd want her to see.

I started coming straight from work to check 'em. I noticed every hole in every leaf. I picked off bugs, pulled out weeds, and I gave 'em lots of that fertilizer called Tomato Food, like somebody told me. From
15 little green marbles, those tomatoes started growing. Then they started getting orange. Then they went to red. I kept looking up at Lateesha's window, wanting her to see it too. The only faces looking back were the drunks that hang out under her place. That liquor store's all boarded up, but they still suck on their bottles there anyway. They liked to call
20 me "field slave" and "share-cropper." Ask how Massa's crops is doing. I could have banged their heads together and shut 'em up, but I didn't. That was part of the point of the tomatoes. I was showing Lateesha that just cause I got muscles don't mean I'm some jungle beast. I stopped working out and stopped going out with no shirt, no matter how hot it
25 was. When some chicks would be walking by and see me there and say "Looking fine," I knew they meant me but I'd point to my biggest tomato and say back "Sure is." My homies all laughed to see me out there. Stopped calling me Ceps. Started in calling me Tomato. I just smiled.
30 Those tomatoes got big as billiard balls. One day when I checked 'em, my biggest one, the one I'd been watching closest, was gone. The

---

6 **bud** flower before it opens up *(Knospe)* – 8 **stake** pole – 9 **disease** [dɪ'zi:z] illness –
10 **blight** plant disease – 14 **fertilizer** "food" for plants *(Dünger)* – 15 **marble** small ball
of colored glass used by children in games *(Murmel)* – 18 **liquor** ['lɪkə] alcohol –
20 **sharecropper** person (often black) who farms land belonging to s.o. else and who
gets part of the crop in return for his work – **Massa** *(southern black speech)* master –
24 **to work out** to do exercises (in a gym) – 25 **chick** *(slang)* girl – 27 **homies** *(slang)*
friends

next day, another one gone. It wasn't insects that took 'em. I was mad. They weren't even all the way ripe yet. My plants were right there by the sidewalk. I put chicken wire around 'em, and even on top, but people could still reach in if they tried. I couldn't guard 'em day and night.
5 Then Royce showed up, just in time.

You drop bread on the ground and birds come out of nowhere. Same with that garden. People just appeared, people you didn't know were there. Royce was like that. Except that he didn't *want* nobody knowing he was there. One of the gardeners saw that her pile of grass clippings
10 was all spread out. Had a sort of human print in it. He'd been sleeping there nights and leaving early. One morning he slept late. I'm the one who found him. He was fifteen, black, built big – looked like I did. His face was banged up. Said his father did it and threw him out. He didn't want to go back. I bought him breakfast and we made us a deal.
15 I found him a place closer to my tomatoes but hidden by somebody's corn, so the cops wouldn't see him sacked out. I bought him a brand new sleeping bag. I gave him money for food that week. Then I picked up a pitchfork for three dollars at a junk shop. His part of the deal was that if he saw or heard *anyone* mess with my tomatoes, he'd come at
20 'em full speed, holding the pitchfork.

That was my best shot protecting 'em at night. For daytime, when Royce was gone, I painted a sign that said "Lateesha's Tomatoes." It was big. I put it right there in front of the plants, facing the sidewalk. If people know something belongs to a person instead of the city or the
25 U.S. government they're more likely to leave it be.

When I'd pounded it in, I filled up my water can. Walking back, I looked up at her window. As still as a cat, behind that lace curtain, there was her face, staring down at the sign.

---

13 **to bang** *(slang) here:* to beat – 16 **sacked out** *(slang)* sleeping in the open – 18 **pitchfork** large fork used for farm work – 19 **to mess with** *(slang)* to do harm – 21 **shot** (sl.) try – 25 **they are likely to** they will probably – 26 **to pound** to hit, to hammer – 27 **lace** netlike ornamental fabric *(Spitze)* – **curtain** fabric covering a window *(Gardine)*

Nora

I always try to get Mr. Myles out for a walk and a taste of fresh air. I don't know about his other nurses. I expect that it's because I'm British. Back in England you'd see mothers pushing infants in prams through winter gales. I expect as well it was the sight of my own father, vegetating in his chair by the fire. We mustn't stop living before our time. So I'm forever telling Mr. Myles.

It was a midsummer morning and I was pushing his wheelchair up Gibb Street, a new route for us. The view, I'll admit, is less than uplifting. Half the storefronts seem to be empty. Mr. Myles must remember a very different scene. His landlady says he's lived here many years. As he lost his speech with his second stroke, he can't tell me himself. He's a mystery. Lately his interest in the world had declined. I'd stop before a store window to let him see himself – he has the dignified head of an African chief – only to find that he'd fallen asleep. I realized that his time might be near. And then, that morning, rolling along the sidewalk, suddenly his arm came up.

He wanted to stop. I obliged him at once. To our left was a lot in which a few bold pioneers had planted gardens. We remained several minutes, watching two Asian women hoeing, then continued on. Immediately, back up went his arm. I came around and looked at him. He twisted and pointed toward the garden. I turned the wheelchair and headed back. I could see his nostrils taking in the smell of the soil. We reached the lot. His arm commanded me to enter. Over the narrow, bumpy path we went, his nose and eyes working. Some remembered scent was pulling him. He was a salmon traveling upstream through his past.

That first day we simply watched the others. We might have been strolling through a miniature city. Some plots sported brick pathways

---

3 **pram** short for: perambulator; push cart for babies – 4 **gale** strong wind – 11 **stroke** sudden illness causing brain damage sometimes leading to the loss of the ability to move some parts of the body *(Schlaganfall)* – 12 **to decline** to decrease *(abnehmen)* – 13 **dignified** ['dɪgnɪfaɪd] proud – 14 **his time might be near** he might die soon – 17 **to oblige s.o.** [ə'blaɪdʒ] to do what s.o. wishes, to help s.o. – 18 **bold** courageous – 19 **to hoe** [həʊ] to remove weeds (with a hoe) – 22 **nostril** ['nɒstrɪl] hole in the nose that allows you to breathe – 25 **scent** [sent] something you can smell – **salmon** ['sæmən] fish with pink meat *(Lachs)* – 28 **to stroll** [strəʊl] to walk leisurely – **to sport** to show openly and with pride

and flower borders, while others looked haphazard. One had a gate that was in fact a car door. Within, beans climbed a propped-up set of bedsprings. A hummingbird feeder, a barbecue grill, a gardening hat hanging from a nail – there were many such domestic touches. I was
5 entranced. I determined that Mr. Myles should do more than simply watch, wheelchair or no.

I worked on the problem in my head. Two days later, driving to his apartment, I stopped at the garden and unloaded a large plastic trash barrel and a shovel. I wheeled him up an hour later, used my pocketknife
10 to cut holes in the bottom of the barrel for drainage, and built up a fine sweat shoveling in dirt. I'd brought with me a dozen seed packets. Mr. Myles chose the flowers decisively, ignoring the vegetables. Was he recalling his mother's flower garden? His history was unknowable. I pushed him as close to the barrel as I could. Thirty minutes later he'd
15 planted hollyhocks, poppies and snapdragons. Riding home afterward, he smelled the dirt on his fingers with satisfaction.

That small circle of earth became a second home to both of us. Gardening boring? Never! It has suspense, tragedy, startling developments – a soap opera growing out of the ground. I'd forgotten
20 that tremolo of expectation produced by a tiny forest of sprouts. What a marvelous sight it was to behold Mr. Myles' furrowed black face inspecting his smooth-skinned young, just arrived in the world he'd shortly leave. His eyes gained back some of their life. He weeded and watered with great concentration. A fact bobbed up from my memory,
25 that the ancient Egyptians prescribed walking through a garden as a cure for the mad. It was a mind-altering drug we took daily.

---

1 **haphazard** [ˌhæpˈhæzəd] unplanned, careless – 2 **to prop up** to put up against –
3 **bedsprings** coiled pieces of wire that make lying in bed comfortable *(Bettfederung)* –
hummingbird *Kolibri* – 4 **domestic** [dəˈmestɪk] having to do with the home *(häuslich)* –
5 **entranced** charmed – 9 **barrel** round container *(Fass)* – 13 **to recall** to remember –
15 **hollyhock** *Stockrose* – **poppy** *Mohnblume* – **snapdragon** *Löwenmäulchen* – 18 **to
startle** to surprise – 20 **tremolo** [ˈtremələʊ] a special, slightly shaking effect produced
by a stringed instrument or a voice – 21 **marvelous** wonderful – **to behold (beheld,
beheld)** to notice, see – **furrowed** wrinkled *(gefurcht)* – 23 **shortly** soon – **to gain** to
win – 24 **to bob up** to come up to the surface – 25 **ancient** [ˈeɪnʃənt] very old – **to
prescribe** [prɪˈskraɪb] to order or give s.th. as a medicine – 26 **mind-altering** changing
a person's psyche

We were rather alone there, off to one side. Our most common visitors were the cats. They were attracted by the aroma of fish, the work of a child who'd copied the Pilgrims of old and buried sardines with her seeds. Then our solitary status ended, as a result of a downpour.
5 When the rain came that day, the other gardeners all ran in the same direction, as if in a fire drill. We followed and found them sheltered beneath a shoe store's overhang two doors down, apparently their customary refuge. The small dry space forced us together. In fifteen minutes we'd met them all and soon knew the whole band of
10 regulars.

Most were old. Many grew plants from their native lands – huge Chinese melons, ginger, cilantro, a green the Jamaicans call calaloo, and many more. Pantomime was often required to get over language barriers. Yet we were all subject to the same weather and pests, the
15 same neighborhood, and the same parental emotions toward our plants. If we happened to miss two or three days, people stopped by on our return to ask about Mr. Myles' health. We, like our seeds, were now planted in the garden.

I told all this to out-of-town guests, then took them up Terminal
20 Tower. We got off at the observation deck on the forty-second floor to find that the garden, which loomed so large to its tenders, was hopelessly hidden from view by buildings. I looked at all the tourists, who'd no notion it existed, who thought they were seeing all of Cleveland, and restrained myself from pointing and shouting out,
25 "The Gibb Street garden is there!"

3 **of old** long ago – 4 **solitary** lonely – **downpour** ['daʊnpɔ:] sudden heavy rain – 6 **to shelter** to protect – 7 **beneath** [bɪ'ni:θ] under – **apparently** [ə'pærəntlɪ] obviously, as it seems – 8 **customary** ['kʌstəmərɪ] normal – **refuge** ['refju:dʒ] place where you are safe *(Zufluchtsort, Schutz)* – 10 **regular** person who normally or regularly does s.th. – 12 **ginger** ['dʒɪndʒə] *Ingwer* – **cilantro** leaves of fresh coriander – 13 **to require** to need – 14 **subject to** depending on – **pests** insects that damage plants – 19 **Terminal Tower** 52-story tower above the terminal of the railroad station in Cleveland – 21 **to loom large** to appear large – **tender** person who looks after s.th. or s.o. – 23 **notion** idea – 24 **to restrain s.o. from doing s.th.** to keep s.o. from doing s.th.

Maricela

If you're Mexican, the Cubans and Puerto Ricans hate you because they think you snuck in illegally and they didn't. Which they would have if they could have walked. If you're a teenager, the whole world hates you. If you're a pregnant teenager, people think you should be
5 burned at the stake. I'm a Mexican, pregnant sixteen-year-old. So shoot me and get it over with.

I wouldn't actually care if you did. In a way I'm already dead. I used to be really, really hot. Because of the baby I'm as fat as a wrestler, I dropped out, I've been to exactly zero parties, and I've been asked out
10 exactly zero times, including by the scum who got me pregnant. My parents were mad. They wanted me to graduate. But abortion or adoption – forget it. Then they got sort of excited about it. They both love little babies. Not me. They started praying for it every night, while I was begging my body to miscarry.

15 Three of us from my high school got into this program for pregnant teens. They give you rides to the doctor and help with getting your G.E.D. at home. Great. Except that Penny, the woman we see, saw the community garden and got the program its own spot, to give us practice taking care of something and to let us witness "the miracle of
20 life." And to try to keep us from eating our babies alive or dropping them into dumpsters.

It was already the middle of summer, so she had us plant radishes since they grow fast. All three of us hate radishes. As soon as the little green leaves came up a gopher or something wiped 'em out. So much
25 for the miracle of life. I didn't tell Penny I was hoping the same thing

2 **to sneak in (snuck, snuck)** to enter (the country) secretly – 4 **pregnant** having an unborn baby inside – 5 **stake** a post to which a person was tied in former times to be killed by being burned – 8 **hot** *here:* good-looking, pretty – 9 **to drop out** to leave high school before having finished it – 10 **scum** unpleasant, nasty person – 11 **to graduate** to finish high school with a diploma – **abortion** medical operation in which a baby's development inside a woman is stopped – 14 **to beg** to ask in an urgent way – **to miscarry** to lose an unborn child – 17 **G.E.D.** a test administered by the general education development for adults who have dropped out of high school – **the woman we see** the woman in charge of our program – 21 **dumpster** large metal container used for waste – 24 **gopher** [ˈgəʊfə] rat-like animal living in holes in the ground *(Erdeichhörnchen)*

happened to my baby. She's so cheerful I never could. *She*'s not puking or getting as big as a blimp – *no wonder* she's always smiling.

After the radishes came squash, then Swiss chard, which nobody knew how to eat. I was in my seventh month. I hated the bending. We all complained, but Penny just smiled. The rest of us called working there the Chain Gang. I hated the feel of dirt under my nails. One afternoon Yolanda broke two of her fancy, painted, expensive nails and cursed out loud for ten minutes. Penny couldn't shut her up. Then another woman came over and gave us this long lecture about the word "decorum". I couldn't believe my eyes – it was my old third-grade teacher, Miss Fleck. I prayed she wouldn't recognize me, but naturally she did, and asked me all the usual questions. I should have had the answers printed up on a card to hand out. The next week, when some man threw a can out his window, which landed about a foot from my head, Miss Fleck figured out what apartment he was in, walked up, and yelled at him like he was a kid. She treated the whole world like her classroom.

Different people came to our part of the garden for different reasons. This Puerto Rican kid had these pumpkin plants that kept getting into ours. Which gave him an excuse to walk right past me and talk to Dolores, who was fifteen and pretty and still didn't look pregnant. I couldn't wait for her to get huge. Sometimes this black guy ran through our garden. He couldn't take time to go around. He grew lettuce, or tried to. Most of it was dead. He'd drive up on a cab, slam on the brakes like the Pope just stepped in front of him, run through our squash, cut a bunch of lettuce, and run back with it in a bucket of water. Then he'd peel out, leaving lots of rubber. Then there were the people who came by to give us different things. Vegetables that they'd grown and thought we should eat, which we always gave away later. Advice on growing our

---

2 **to puke** to throw up; to bring food back from your stomach through your mouth – **blimp** an airship shaped somewhat like an egg – 3 **squash** *(AE)* vegetable similar to a pumpkin – **Swiss chard** [tʃɑːd] vegetable with large leaves *(Mangold)* – 6 **Chain Gang** *(U.S.)* group of criminals who were forced to work chained to each other – 8 **to curse** to use bad language – 10 **decorum** [dɪˈkɔːrəm] correct behavior showing respect – 24 **to slam on the brakes** to stop a car very abruptly – 27 **to peel out** *here:* to make a sudden start

stupid Swiss chard. Advice on giving birth and raising kids, which I tuned out as soon as they started.

One day in August it was just me and Penny. This black woman, Leona, who had a garden and talked to us, came over and gave me
5 some flowers she'd grown. They were yellow. She called 'em goldenrod and she said if I made 'em into tea it would help me with the delivery. She knew I didn't want to be pregnant. I could talk to her about it. That day it was almost too humid to talk. The windows around the garden were open and you could hear ten different TV's and radios. A storm
10 was coming. The thunder was getting closer. And then it hit – *bam*! Then all the TV's and radios went off. So did the lights. It was a power failure.

It was quiet in the garden without all the noise. So quiet it was weird. I looked around. An old man near us was slowly picking cucumbers,
15 like nothing had happened. "Whole city shuts down, but the garden just keeps going," Leona said. She talked on, how plants don't run on electricity or clock time, how none of nature did. How nature ran on sunlight and rain and the seasons, and how I was part of that system. The words sort of put me into a daze. My body was part of nature. I was
20 related to bears, to dinosaurs, to plants, to things that were a million years old. It hit me that this system was much older and stronger than the other. She said how it wasn't some disgrace to be part of it. She said it was an honor. I stared at the squash plants. It was a world in there. It seemed like I could actually see the leaves and flowers growing and
25 changing. I was in that weird daze. And for just that minute I stopped wishing my baby would die.

---

2 **to tune s.th. out** to shut your ears to s.th., to stop showing interest in s.th. –
6 **delivery** *here:* the act of giving birth to a baby – 8 **humid** ['hju:mɪd] opposite of dry;
here: close *(schwül)* – 11 **power failure** breakdown of the electricity supply – 13 **weird**
strange – 14 **cucumber** ['kju:k͜mbə] long vegetable with green skin *(Gurke)* –19 **daze**
dreamlike state, state of confusion *(Benom-menheit)* – 22 **disgrace** s.th. shameful

Amir

In India we have many vast cities, just as in America. There, too, you are one among millions. But there at least you know your neighbors. Here, one cannot say that. The object in America is to avoid contact, to treat all as foes unless they're known to be friends. Here you have a
5 million crabs living in a million crevices.

When I saw the garden for the first time, so green among the dark brick buildings, I thought back to my parents' Persian rug. It showed climbing vines, rivers and waterfalls, grapes, flower beds, singing birds, everything a desert dweller might dream of. Those rugs were indeed
10 portable gardens. In the summers in Delhi, so very hot, my sisters and I would lie upon it and try to press ourselves into its world. The garden's green was as soothing to the eye as the deep blue of that rug. I'm aware of color – I manage a fabric store. But the garden's greatest benefit, I feel, was not relief to the eyes, but to make the eyes see our
15 neighbors.

I grew eggplants, onions, carrots, and cauliflower. When the eggplants appeared in August they were pale purple, a strange and eerie shade. When my wife would bring our little son, he was forever wanting to pick them. There was nothing else in the garden with that
20 color. Very many people came over to ask about them and talk to me. I recognized a few from the neighborhood. Not one had spoken to me before – and now how friendly they turned out to be. The eggplants gave them an excuse for breaking the rules and starting a conversation. How happy they seemed to have found this excuse, to let their natural
25 friendliness out.

Those conversations tied us together. In the middle of summer someone dumped a load of tires on the garden at night, as if it were still

---

1 **vast** [vɑːst] very large, huge – 3 **to avoid** to keep away from – 4 **foe** enemy – 5 **crab** sea creature with a hard shell and ten legs *(Krebs)* – **crevice** ['krevɪs] narrow opening or crack in a rock or wall – 7 **rug** carpet – 8 **vine** Weinrebe, Kletterpflanze – **grape** Weintraube – 9 **dweller** inhabitant – 10 **portable** which can be carried around – 12 **to soothe** to calm – **to be aware of** be conscious of, to know about – 13 **fabric** ['fæbrɪk] cloth *(Stoff)* – **benefit** ['benəfɪt] advantage, s.th. good – 14 **relief** removal of pain *(Erleichterung)* – 16 **eggplant** Aubergine – **cauliflower** Blumenkohl – 17 **pale** not bright *(blass)* – 18 **eerie** strange, causing a feeling of fear and mystery – 23 **excuse** *here:* a reason for doing s.th. *(Ausrede)* – 27 **tire** *(BE spelling: tyre)* rubber part of a car wheel

filled with trash. A man's four rows of young corn were crushed. In an hour, we had all the tires by the curb. We were used to helping each other by then. A few weeks later, early in the evening a woman screamed, down the block from the garden. A man with a knife had
5 taken her purse. Three men from the garden ran after him. I was surprised that I was one of them. Even more surprising, we caught him. Royce held the man to a wall with his pitchfork until the police arrived. I asked the others. Not one of us had ever chased a criminal before. And most likely we wouldn't have except near the garden.
10 There, you felt part of a community.

I came to the United States in 1980. Cleveland is a city of immigrants. The Poles are especially well known here. I'd always heard that the Polish men were tough steelworkers and that the women cooked lots of cabbage. But I'd never known one – until the garden. She was an old
15 woman whose space bordered mine. She had a seven-block walk to the garden, the same route I took. We spoke quite often. We both planted carrots. When her hundreds of seedlings came up in a row, I was very surprised that she did not thin them – pulling out all but one healthy-looking plant each few inches, to give them room to grow. I
20 asked her. She looked down at them and said she knew she ought to do it, but that this task reminded her too closely of her concentration camp, where the prisoners were inspected each morning and divided into two lines – the healthy to live and the others to die. Her father, an orchestra violinist, had spoken out against the Germans, which had
25 caused her family's arrest. When I heard her words, I realized how useless was all that I'd heard about Poles, how much richness it hid, like the worthless shell around an almond. I still do not know, or care, whether she cooks cabbage.

The garden found this out with Royce. He was young and black. He
30 looked rather dangerous. People watched him and seemed to be relieved when he left the garden. Then he began spending more time there. We found out that he had a stutter. Then that he had two sisters, that he liked the cats that roamed through the garden, and that he worked very well with his hands. Soon all the mothers were trying to

2 **curb** part of the sidewalk *(Bordstein)* – 5 **purse** *(AE)* handbag – 14 **cabbage** round vegetable with green or purple leaves (Kohl) – 27 **almond** ['ɑːmənd] nut-like fruit *(Mandel)* – 30 **to be relieved** to be happy *(erleichtert sein)* – 32 **stutter** stammer *(Stottern)* – 33 **to roam** to wander about

feed him. How very strange it was to watch people who would have crossed the street if they'd seen him coming a few weeks before, now giving him vegetables, more than he could eat. In return, he watered for people who were sick and fixed fences and made other repairs. He might weed your garden or use the bricks from the building that was torn down up the block to make you a brick path between your rows. He always pretended he hadn't done it. It was always a surprise. One felt honored to be chosen. He was trusted and liked – and famous, after his exploit with the pitchfork. He was not a black teenage boy. He was Royce.

In September he and a Mexican man collected many bricks from up the street and built a big barbecue. I was in the garden on Saturday when the Mexican family drove up in a truck with a dead pig in the back. They built a fire, put a heavy metal spit through the pig, and began to roast it. A bit later their friends began arriving. One brought a guitar, another played violin. They filled a folding table with food. Perhaps it was one of their birthdays, or perhaps no reason was needed for the party. It was beautiful weather, sunny but not hot. Fall was just beginning and the garden was changing from green to brown. Those of us who had come to work felt the party's spirit enter us. The smell of the roasting pig drifted out and called to everyone, gardeners or not. Soon the entire garden was filled.

It was a harvest festival, like those in India, though no one had planned it to be. People brought food and drinks and drums. I went home to get my wife and son. Watermelons from the garden were sliced open. The gardeners proudly showed off what they'd grown. We traded harvests, as we often did. And we gave food away, as we often did also – even I, a businessman, trained to give away nothing, to always make a profit. The garden provided many excuses for breaking that particular rule.

Many people spoke to me that day. Several asked where I was from. I wondered if they knew as little about Indians as I had known about Poles. One old woman, Italian I believe, said she'd admired my eggplants for weeks and told me how happy she was to meet me. She praised them and told me how to cook them and asked all about my

---

9 **exploit** ['eksplɔɪt] brave, exciting act – 14 **spit** long, thin metal rod put through meat when roasting it – 18 **fall** *(AE)* autumn – 27 **to trade** to exchange – **harvest** *here:* the fruits and vegetables harvested

family. But something bothered me. Then I remembered. A year before she'd claimed that she'd received the wrong change in my store. I was called out to the register. She'd gotten quite angry and called me – despite her own accent – a dirty foreigner. Now that we were so friendly
5 with each other I dared to remind her of this. Her eyes became huge. She apologized to me over and over again. She kept saying, "Back then, I didn't know it was *you* ..."

1 **to bother** to make s.o. mad – 3 **register** cash register *(Registrierkasse)* – 6 **to apologize** [əˈpɒlədʒaɪz] to say that one is sorry

Florence

My great-grandparents walked all the way from Louisiana to Colorado.
That was in 1859. They were both freed slaves and they wanted to get
good and far from cotton-growing country. They went over the
mountains, just to be safe, and homesteaded along the Gunnison
River. Which is how my grandfather and my father and my sisters and
I all came to be born there, the first black family in the whole country.
My father called them our seedfolks, because they were the first of our
family there.

I think of them when I see any of the people who started the garden
on Gibb Street. They're seedfolks too. I'm talking about that first year,
before there were spigots and hoses, and the toolshed, and new soil.
And before the landlords started charging more for apartments that
look on the garden.

I would have been in on the garden for sure if it weren't for this
arthritis in my hands. Growing up out in the country, I still miss country
things. My husband's from here. He doesn't know about the smell of a
hayfield and eating beans off the vine instead of from the store. I had
to settle for being a watcher. I wasn't the only one. I'd see others on the
fire escapes, or standing on the sidewalk like me. One day I looked up
and saw a head in a window moving forward and back. It was a man
who'd pulled up his rocking chair. He was watching the gardeners like
TV.

My grandmother's sampler, from when she was a girl, said "Be Not
Solitary, Be Not Idle." That was easy all those years in the library. Being
retired, it's harder. So I try to take a walk every day, which is how I found
the garden to begin with. I'd always stop there, to see what was new. I
was just a watcher, but I was proud of the garden, as if it were mine.

---

4 **to homestead** to find and claim a piece of land in the U.S. west – **Gunnison River**
river in central Colorado – 11 **spigot** ['spɪgət] tap – **toolshed** wooden cabin that tools
(=*Werkzeuge)* are kept in – 12 **landlord** person owning property (houses, apartments)
and renting it out – **to charge** to ask s.o. to pay – 14 **to be in on s.th.** to take part in
s.th. – **if it weren't for** if I didn't have – 18 **to settle for** to accept – 19 **fire escape** metal
ladder on an outside wall of a building to be used in case of fire – 21 **rocking chair**
chair moving back and forth – 23 **sampler** piece of cloth decorated with different
stitches often displayed on a wall *(Stickmustertuch)* – 24 **idle** ['aɪdl] inactive, lazy –
25 **retired** no longer working

Proud and protective. I remember how mad I got when I saw a man reach through someone's fence by the sidewalk and try to grab a tomato. I said "How dare you!" He pulled back his hand and said he'd heard it was a *community* garden.

5 It's sad every fall, seeing it turn brown. Fewer and fewer people there. That very first year was the hardest. It had been such a wonderful change to see people making something for themselves instead of waiting for a welfare check. To see a part of the neighborhood looking *better* every day, and to smell those good smells of growing plants. The
10 green drained away. Then the frost hit. You'd pass and hear those dry cornstalks shaking in the wind as if they were shivering. The pumpkins were about the only color left, and then the boy sold them all. Some people cut up their old plants with clippers and dug them back into the soil. A few covered their ground with leaves. But once that job was
15 done, it was done. By November the cats were the only ones there.

That winter was a cold one. Cold as Colorado. You'd walk by the garden, covered with snow, just the fence tops sticking out, and you'd try to remember it back in July. Someone stuck a Christmas tree there in December. It stayed up until March. It's hard to tell one month from
20 another that time of year. It's all just winter. Because of the weather I missed lots of walks. When I did get out, I couldn't go past the garden without slowing down to look, even though there was nothing growing. Sometimes there'd be one of the gardeners there, just looking too.

You can't see Canada across Lake Erie, but you know it's there. It's the
25 same with spring. You have to have faith, especially in Cleveland. Snow in April always breaks your heart. I think we had two April snows that year. Waiting for the snow to melt was like waiting for a glacier to move. Finally, it was gone for good. The ground was back, and last year's leaves, like a bookmark showing where you'd left off. It was a joy to get

---

1 **to be protective** to look after, to keep danger away from – 8 **welfare check** *(A.E.)* financial help given to the poor – 10 **to drain away** to disappear – 11 **cornstalk** stem supporting corn cobs *(Maisstengel)* – **to shiver** [ˈʃɪvə] to shake because it is cold – 13 **clippers** tool used for cutting plants – 21 **to miss s.th.** *here:* to not do s.th. – 25 **faith** trust, belief – 27 **glacier** [ˈglæsɪə] mass of ice formed by snow on mountains – 28 **for good** forever – 29 **bookmark** piece of paper showing the reader where he/she has stopped reading

out again. Just to walk without wearing a heavy coat and boots felt like flying. But the garden was still empty. I was disappointed. I suppose it was still too early to plant. I began to wonder if anyone would come. Maybe no one was interested. Or maybe the city had shut it down, or sold the lot. I was worried. Then one day I passed it – and someone was digging.

It was a little Oriental girl, with a trowel and a plastic bag of lima beans. I didn't recognize her. It didn't matter. I felt as happy inside as if I'd just seen the first swallow of spring. Then I looked up. There was the man in the rocker.

We waved and waved to each other.

---

9 **swallow** bird with narrow pointed wings and forked tail *(Schwalbe)* – 10 **rocker** rocking chair

Supplementary Texts

1. Blighted U.S. Neighborhoods Blooming

CHICAGO– With the historic drop in violent crime beginning to take hold in even the most blighted urban areas, cities across the United States are being transformed as neighborhoods that had become frightening wastelands are showing glimmers of renaissance.

5 From Boston to New Orleans and Los Angeles to Miami, neighborhoods where drug gangs controlled the streets, commandeered empty houses and terrorized residents are slowly beginning to seem safer and more livable, according to interviews with people in nine cities that have seen sharp drops in violent crime.

10 New homes are being built, stores are opening, subway and bus lines are adding service, and banks and shopping strips are breaking ground. There is less graffiti and fewer abandoned cars and vacant lots. For the first time in years, people are sitting on their front porches and parents feel safe letting their children walk to school. [...]

15 Experts say such progress results from a number of social and economic factors. The booming economy has created so much urban development that builders and businesses are venturing farther away from well-established neighborhoods into ones that were once on the edge of livability.

20 Cities are using budget surpluses to offer tax incentives to businesses that open in these areas. And in some places, like Chicago, other major changes are under way in these commu-nities, including changes in schools and the dismantling of huge, crime-plagued housing projects.

25 With less crime, there have been more jobs [...]

"Investors are starting to feel more comfortable," Mr. Nero [president of the Beacon Council, a private nonprofit economic development agency] said. "The more investment you have in an area the safer it is and the safer it will become."

---

blighted damaged, ruined, slum-like – 1 **historic** famous or important event – **drop** decline, decrease – **to take hold** to become effective or noticeable – 4 **glimmer** a faint unsteady light; a small sign – 6 **to commandeer** to take private property without paying – 11 **to break ground** to begin construction – 20 **budget surpluses** extra money not yet spent – **incentive** encouragement

Also, as things improve and as new policing strategies concentrate on community outreach, residents have become more willing to cooperate with police and that cooperation has helped reduce crime.

By Pam Belluck from The New York Times, reprinted in *International Herald Tribune*, May 30, 2000.

2. Three Poems

Emily Dickinson: A Bird

A bird came down the walk,
5 He did not know I saw;
He bit an angleworm in halves
And ate the fellow, raw.

And then he drank a dew
From a convenient grass,
10 And then hopped sidewise to the wall
To let a beetle pass.

Robert Graves: The Pumpkin

You may not believe it, for hardly could I:
I was cutting a pumpkin to put in a pie,
And on it was written in letters most plain
15 "You may hack me in slices, but I´ll grow again."

I seized it and sliced it and made no mistake
As, with dough rounded over, I put it to bake:
But soon in the garden as I chanced to walk,
Why, there was that pumpkin entire on its stalk!

From *Collected Poems* (1975) by Robert Graves, reprintd by permission of Carcanet Press Limited.

---

2 **community outreach** services provided by the city
Emily Dickinson (1830 - 1886): 8 **dew** tiny drops of water *(Tau)* – 9 **convenient** *here:* easily reached
Robert Graves (1895 - 1985): 14 **plain** easy to see – 17 **dough** mixture of flour, water, etc. *(Teig)* – 19 **entire** whole

Anonymous: Four seasons

Spring is showery, flower, bowery.
Summer: hoppy, croppy, poppy.
Autumn: wheezy, sneezy, freezy.
Winter slippy, drippy, nippy.

3. Starting a Community Garden

All across America people have joined together to turn ugly lots into
beautiful gardens. You may not imagine that you can do it – but you
can. If there is already a community garden in your neighborhood, ask
your neighbors how they got started. But if you are the first on your
5 block to "make something happen," this is what you can do:

1. Find an interested grown-up who wants to help you: a parent or
guardian, a teacher, a librarian, or a neighbor.

2. Find out the address of the lot. This is very important. You may have
to talk to neighbors or look at the address of the buildings next door.
10 Example: The lot I am interested in is on Main Street. It is between 75
Main Street and 81 Main Street.

3. While you are finding out the address of the lot, get in touch with the
local gardening program in your area (see end of this note). Say that
you are interested in starting a garden. Since every city is different,
15 your local program will be able to steer you in the right direction.

4. Find out who the owner is. The Department of Records at your local
city hall can help. Look in the telephone book for the address of city
hall in your area.

5. If the lot is owned by the city, the people at city hall can help you get
20 permission to use the lot. Usually there is a small fee. If the lot is owned

---

7 **guardian** person chosen by a court to be in charge of a child (Vormund) – 15 **to steer**
to direct, to point – 16 **Department of Records** *Katasteramt* – 20 **fee** sum of money to
be paid in exchange for the right to do s.th.

by an individual person or group, you will need to get permission from
that person or group to use the lot.

6. Once you get permission to use the lot, it's yours to name!

There are hundreds of gardening programs that are ready to help community gardeners with information, soil, seeds, fencing, and more.

To find out the community gardening program that is nearest you,
write to: American Community Gardening Association
        300 N. 20th Street, 5th Floor
        Philadelphia, PA 19103-1495

Community gardens bring people together. Join the work and join the
fun!

From City Green by DyAnne DiSalvo-Ryan, New York: William Morrow, 1994.
Copyright © 1994 by DyAnne DiSalvo-Ryan.

4. The Secret Garden

*Mary, who has been sent to her uncle's Yorkshire manor house from
India, is a spoilt orphaned girl who hates and is unfriendly to everybody.
However, she undergoes a transformation when a robin helps her discover the key to a hidden garden, which becomes her favourite playground. With the help of Dickon, a boy who relates to the animal world
in an extraordinary way, the gardener Ben Weatherstaff and Mrs Medlock, the housekeeper, she grows to like the garden and starts to grow
plants in it. Finally she causes her uncle's son Colin, who is believed to
be crippled for life and terminally ill, to recover from his illness by taking him out into the garden and by having him discover its beauties. In
the scene printed here Colin's father inquires about his son's strange
trans-formation.*

"How is Master Colin, Medlock?" he inquired.

    "Well, sir," Mrs Medlock answered, "he's – he's different, in a manner
of speaking."

    "Worse?" he suggested.

    Mrs Medlock really was flushed.

"Well, you see, sir," she tried to explain, "neither Dr Craven, nor the nurse, nor me can exactly make him out."

"Why is that?"

"To tell you the truth, sir, Master Colin might be better and he might
5 be changing for the worse. His appetite, sir, is past understanding – and his ways – "

"Has he become – more peculiar?" Her master asked, knitting his brows anxiously.

"That's it sir. He's growing very peculiar – when you compare him
10 with what he used to be. He used to eat nothing and then suddenly he began to eat something enormous – and then he stopped again all at once and the meals were sent back just as they used to be. You never knew, sir, perhaps, that out of doors he never would let himself be taken. The things we've gone through to get him to go out in his chair
15 would leave a body trembling like a leaf. He'd throw himself into such a state that Dr Craven said he couldn't be responsible for forcing him. Well, sir, just without warning – not long after one of his worst tantrums – he suddenly insisted on being taken out every day by Miss Mary and Susan Sowerby's boy Dickon that could push his chair. He
20 took a fancy to both Miss Mary and Dickon, and Dickon brought his tame animals, and, if you'll credit it, sir, out of doors he will stay from morning until night."

"How does he look?" was the next question.

"If he took his food natural, sir, you'd think he was putting on flesh
25 – but we're afraid it might be a sort of bloat. He laughs sometimes in a queer way when he's alone with Miss Mary. He never used to laugh at all. Dr Craven is coming to see you at once, if you'll allow him. He never was as puzzled in his life."

"Where is Master Colin now?" Mr Craven asked.

30 "In the garden, sir. He's always in the garden – though not a human creature is allowed to go near for fear they'll look at him."

"In the garden," he said, and after he had sent Mrs. Medlock away he stood and repeated it again and again. "In the Garden!"

From Frances Hodgson Burnett, The Secret Garden, New York: Grosset & Dunlap, pp. 298f.

---

5 **past understanding** impossible to understand – 7 **peculiar** strange – 11 **something enormous** a lot, very much – 16 **state** condition – 17 **tantrum** a fit of bad temper – 21 **if you'll credit it** if you can believe it – 25 **bloat** unhealthy swelling

5 Esperanza Community Garden

There are almost no public spaces in [New York City]. Socializing is based around cafés, bars, restaurants, and shopping — private spaces where you need to pay a fee (whether a cup of coffee or drink) to stay. They are commercial spaces designed to make a profit. And if you can-
5 not afford endless four-dollar cappuccinos or seven-dollar drinks, you find yourself with not a lot of places to go. Even the public parks — which there are not many of — are full of venders, fences, and curfews. And I rarely have an encounter with someone else in the park.

That's why I was amazed to find myself sitting in front of a campfire
10 in a garden in the middle of Manhattan one night this winter, sur-rounded by strangers who were talking to me as though I were sitting in their own kitchen. The garden was called El Jardín de la Esperanza, Spanish for "The Garden of Hope." It was a community garden on the Lower East Side, a garden created and enjoyed by neighbors. It was
15 destroyed by the city of New York.

Many of the gardens on the Lower East Side began in the 1970s. At that time the neighborhood was full of empty lots left by buildings burnt to the ground by landlords when the housing market crashed. These lots were full of trash and debris from the crumbled buildings,
20 and the city made no effort to reuse them. The rubble-strewn lots threatened the safety of children and demoralized the residents.

The people in the community decided to do something about the situation. They went out and reclaimed the land that the city was wast-ing, clearing away the rubble to make room for something new and
25 entirely their own. They cleaned up the trash, prepared the soil, and planted seeds. One by one, the old abandoned lots were covered in new greenery.

---

1 **to socialize** to meet other people – 3 **fee** a sum of money paid in exchange for the right to do s.th. – 4 **designed** arranged in such a way – 5 **to afford** to have the money to do s.th. – 7 **vender** person who sells s.th. – **curfew** time at night after which certain people are no longer allowed outside (*here:* time after which parks are closed at night) – 8 **encounter** meeting – 14 **Lower East Side** the southeastern part of Manhattan – 18 **to crash** to collapse, to lose its profitability – 19 **debris** ['debri:] broken remains of a building – 20 **rubble-strewn** covered with trash – 23 **to reclaim** to make useful again

Esperanza was one of the most active community gardens developed in this period. It was planted in 1977 by Alicia Torres, her family, and the neighbors who lived next door to the empty lot at 221 East 7th Street. It took them an entire year to clear the trash and prepare the
5 ground, but the result was well worth the effort.

The birth of the gardens helped to transform the Lower East Side from a burnt-out ghetto into a vibrant, attractive community. This new beauty became a double-edged sword, though, because by the early 1980s the neighborhood began to attract real estate developers. New
10 York City's government created the cross-subsidy plan, which allowed the gardens to be sold off for luxury develop-ments as long as a small, flexible percentage of the housing was designated for low-income tenants.

Housing is a pressing concern in New York City. However, what is
15 being built is primarily luxury rate housing, with rents out of reach of the people who actually live in the Lower East Side. And the city targeted lots where the gardens were growing for develop-ment, even though there are plenty of vacant lots available in the same neighborhoods, often on the same streets. Esperanza was one of these gar-
20 dens.

[Esperanza Garden was bulldozed on February 15, 2000. This happened by order of the administration of the City of New York. More than 150 garden supporters occupied the garden and 31 of them were arrested for refusing to leave.]

From the article "Saving Esperanza Garden" by Kerstin Mikalbrown
http://www.pdflibrary.org/pdf/saving-esperanza-garden-the-struggle-over-community.html

9 **real estate developer** person or firm that creates new housing − 12 **tenant** person who rents an apartment